F777
.6
.F5
1914

To Officers and Members of Organized Labor:

Dear Sirs and Brothers:

"The Ludlow Massacre," by Walter H. Fink, our publicity agent, is an authentic and interesting narrative of the sufferings of Colorado coal miners, their wives and children.

Mr. Fink has been in active touch with the situation since before the strike and with his experience as our publicity agent, there is none better able to write a story of the struggle. We believe so thoroughly in the ability of Mr. Fink to write the real story of the strike that we have had him at work for the past eight months compiling a history of our fight in Colorado since 1876.

"The Ludlow Massacre" is being sold at twenty-five cents, a little more than cost, that every worker in the country may be fully acquainted with the horrors of the Colorado strike and we believe you will find it well worth reading.

Thanking you for your enthusiastic support of our strike, we are

Yours very truly,
JOHN R. LAWSON,
JOHN McLENNAN,
E. L. DOYLE,
Policy Committee District 15, U. M. W. A.

Introduction

"The Ludlow Massacre" gives the workers of the country the first complete and authentic story of the horrors of the Colorado coal miners' strike.

. Sixty-six persons are known to have been killed and forty-eight wounded in the numerous battles and disorders since the miners went on strike, September 23, 1913. Classified, eighteen strikers, ten mine guards, nineteen mine employes, two militiamen, three non-combatants, two women and twelve children lost their lives. Twenty had been killed prior to April 20, the date of the massacre at Ludlow, and forty-six were killed during the next ten days, until federal troops stopped the warfare.

The cost of the eight months' industrial conflict is estimated at $15,000,000. The figures include $700,000, representing the state's expense in maintaining state troops in the field until the arrival of the federal forces; an estimated cost of $6,925,000 to the union, and a loss of "several millions" claimed by the operators.

It seems impossible that here in supposedly free America, men, women and children must be slaughtered, mothers with babes in their arms must be ridden down and maimed by a man like Adjutant General Chase, a pliant lickspittle of the operators; that the motherhood of the nation must submit to robbery,, abuse and fiendish outrages; that men and women must forego their right of trial by jury and other injustices that they may force the capitalist-owned state and county executives to enforce the laws and re-establish constitutional government. But the fact remains that the Colorado miners have suffered all of these things that they might secure an enforcement of state laws.

WALTER H. FINK.

MOTHER JONES

82-Year-Old Angel of the Coal Camps, who was denied her constitutional rights in Colorado and imprisoned, incommunicado, in a vermin-ridden, rat-infested cell.

The Ludlow Massacre

It was Sunday afternoon.

The Greek members of the Ludlow tent colony were celebrating their Easter.

John D. Rockefeller, Jr., had just preached the word of God to his Sunday school class in New York City.

The strikers and their families were enjoying themselves at a baseball game. They were a happy, care-free audience of twenty-one nationalities, thinking of nothing but the freedom from industrial and political slavery that they were willingly purchasing by an incessant war with the elements, with the imported assassins of John D. Rockefeller, with the corporation-owned state and county officials of Colorado.

It had been a day of joy, a day such as victory in the strike will bring them every twenty-four hours of the future.

The baseball game was almost over when down out of the hills, where these strikers had lived in hovels like hogs, had been robbed of their coal, had been deprived of their political, industrial and religious liberty, had been driven into unsafe mines to be slaughtered, came the gunmen of industry, the hired murderers of Sunday school teacher and "philanthropist" John D. Rockefeller, Jr.

There were five of these gunmen on horseback and armed with high-power rifles. They came to break up the baseball game. But they realized that even high-powered rifles and machine guns trained on the baseball diamond from the hills might not be able to combat the crowd of fans, and they started away chagrined.

Some of the strikers' wives and children laughed at these imported assassins who were too cowardly to carry out their purpose.

"Oh, that's all right; have your fun today; we'll

have our roast tomorrow," said one of the gunmen, and they rode away.

Little did these peaceful men, women and children realize the horrible prophecy this thug was making.

They were accustomed to the intimidation of these gunmen. They knew that these derelicts were hired to murder them, but not for a moment did they imagine that "our roast tomorrow," as threatened by the gunmen, was to be their cremation.

They did not know that the gunmen militiamen had trained six machine guns on the Ludlow tent colony the night before. They did not know that these same murderers of the State of Colorado and John D. Rockefeller had completely surrounded the camp. They did not know that their massacre was only a question of when three bombs should be exploded at the headquarters of Major Hamrock.

April 20th dawned a typical morning for the strikers. Men were busy with their chores. Here and there throughout the tent colony could be heard the merry little song of the washboard. Children darted here and there out of the tents, happy, playful 300 tots, not knowing that before the sun had set they were to go through the most terrible holocaust in the history of industrial struggles. In the rear of Snodgrass' store men and boys were playing baseball.

Since last September these people had been taught nothing but peace. Their leaders had told them day after day that they could never hope to make the disinterested citizen understand their side of the controversy unless they strictly obeyed every law and "attended to their own business."

Men in every walk of life who have investigated the strike or spent any time in the district have talked of the almost ultra-conservatism of the union officials. The men and women and children of the tent colonies had absorbed this feeling of obeyance to the laws. They had patiently suffered the intimidation and tortures of the gunmen and militiamen.

It was 9:55 o'clock that morning when the strikers and their wives and children were thrown into a panic of fear by the explosion of a bomb at the tent of Major Hamrock. It was the signal to the gunmen miltiamen, surrounding the camp on all sides, that it was time to start the massacre of the innocents of Ludlow and destroy the tent colony.

There were not more than forty rifles in the tent colony. The men owning these scattered to the hills in a vain effort to draw the fire of the attacking party and save their loved ones.

At 10 o'clock a second bomb was exploded. Ten seconds later the third shot was fired and the slaughter of Ludlow began.

Massacre of the Innocents.

None will know the agonies of that day.

From surrounding hills poured a criss-cross rain of bullets from machine guns and high-powered rifles.

Tents were riddled with bullets until they looked like so many fishing nets.

Using the machine guns like garden hose, the gunmen cut down everything that rose in their path of death as they swerved from one end of the colony to the other and back again.

Women, driven almost insane, ran like frightened hares into caves dug for their safety, their babes clutching frantically at their breasts, their older children tearing at their skirts, while around them fell the explosive bullets of the gunmen-militiamen.

Quarter was given none by these assassins. They had been hired at $3 to $7 a day to do this dastardly work of exterminating the strikers, and they were determined to do it well.

Into caves, cellars, wells, deserted buildings and

PICTURE OF ONE OF THE MACHINE GUNS MOWING DOWN THE MEN, WOMEN AND CHILDREN AT LUDLOW across the open prairie fled frantic mothers and children.

One well near the tent colony was packed with a hysterical, seething mass that might at any minute be slaughtered.

Out of one of these safety retreats ran little Frankie Snyder, 11 years old, to get a drink of water for his mother and little sisters, who had become ill from fright. He was shot through the head and killed instantly.

Throughout the day Louis Tikas, leader of the Greeks, braved the hail of explosive bullets, going here and there through the tents, rescuing women and children and taking them to places of safety.

Tikas finally saw that it was impossible to save all of the women and children unless the firing stopped. He called Major Hamrock, saloonkeeper in charge of Colorado's uniformed murderers, and arranged for a meeting.

Tikas a Murdered Hero.

Tikas never returned from that conference.

He was taken prisoner. Some of the gunmen wanted to hang this refined, law-abiding Greek. But before they could carry out their purpose, Linderfelt, more bloodthirsty, hit Tikas on the head, crushing his skull and killing him instantly. Linderfelt has admitted that he hit Tikas, breaking the stock of his gun on the Greek's head.

While the Greek lay on the ground dead, another cut-throat kicked him in the face. And then, to cover up this terrible murder, they shot him in the back, giving out the story that he was killed when he tried to escape. One of the bullets exploded in his stomach, the jacket lodging under the skin and the bullet tearing its way through his abdomen.

James Fyler, secretary of the Ludlow union, was another striker who was murdered while a prisoner of the Hamrock-Linderfelt "militiamen"

Fyler was one of the real heroes of that day. With his life in danger every minute, he remained at the telephone, giving the world the only news of the horror. He was shot with an explosive bullet, which blew out the front of his face. When his body was found, $300 which he had in his pocket that morning was missing.

Another of the heroes was Charles Costa. When the gunmen militia started their murderous assault, he, with others in the tent colony who had guns, ran to the hills to do all he could to save the women and children and their homes.

Costa was one of the five men of Ludlow colony to pay the penalty of death for fighting for his constitutional rights, thus defying the rule of anarchy established by Governor Ammons, Adjutant General John Chase and others of the operators' tools who hold office in Colorado.

Costa was shot through the head. As he lay there, in view of his tented home where women and children were being murdered and cremated, dying, he said to his comrades, sing "Union Forever."

Dies Singing Song.

They crowded around him, the bullets stirring up the dirt about their feet like a windstorm. Costa joined in the refrain—

"We've whipped them in the North, boys,
    We'll whip them in the South,
    Shouting—"

And Charles Costa was dead. But the smile on his lips showed that he was willing to go.

Had his comrades known what was happening down in the tent colony, they would have given that smile a two-fold meaning. They would have said that he was smiling, too, because of the anticipation of meeting his wife and three little children in Heaven, where Rockefeller's millions do not rule, where it does not mean death to fight for those things which belong to you.

For, while Costa was breathing his last, his wife and three little children were lying dead in the "Black Hole," their bodies burned almost beyond recognition by the oil-fed fire started by Rockefeller's murderers.

Without food, without water, amid a shower of bullets that pierced their places of shelter, the women and children of Ludlow spent that day.

Among them were mothers with babes at their breasts, women who were to become mothers that day and the next and the next.

The militia knew there were no men in these retreats. They knew there were no arms there to return their fusillade of bullets. They knew that in those places there were only women and children, but they were the wives and daughters of "those d— red-necks." In the eyes of the gunmen militia that removed all questions of sex It was sufficient reason to slaughter them if they could.

Refugees peering from their caves, wondering whether this hail of lead would never cease, were paralyzed with fear about 7 o'clock that evening when they saw a militiaman crawl up to a tent on the outskirts of the tent colony and set it afire with a blazing torch.

Slaughtered Babes Cremated.

Like a cyclone, the flames swept over the tented homes, feeding on the oil of Rockefeller which saturated them and seemingly gloating over the feast provided by the women and children whom they burned and roasted and clasped between their jaws of death until they were an inanimate mass of crisp flesh and bones.

Here and there the fire refused to spread and up would spring another assassin with a torch to set it afire.

HAPPY CHILDREN OF THE LUDLOW TENT COLONY

Some of whom were murdered and cremated by Rockefeller's gunmen under command of
Butcher Linderfelt and Saloonkeeper Hamrock.

In small, ill-ventilated caves, in wells, in deserted farm houses, on the open prairie, the women and children of Ludlow spent that night, mourning the loss of fathers, brothers, husbands, of new-born babes, who had come into the world that day only to be murdered and cremated by the Colorado assassins, and all around them fell the bullets of the uniformed murderers.

Nothing so wanton has ever been known as the terrible thirst for blood of these assassins. They knew that these women and children had no food, no water. But they continued their firing with the seeming purpose of driving the famished mothers and tots into the open for food and water that they might also shoot them down.

Probably the most heinous feature of this massacre was the refusal of the militia officers to allow doctors or Red Cross nurses to minister to the wounded.

Physicians who went there under flags of truce soon after the slaughter began, were driven back by bullets.

Flags of the Red Cross Society were shot into shreds with the same utter disregard as the American flag.

Shot at American Flag.

It is not generally known, but it is a matter of fact that the Stars and Stripes—the flag of our nation—was fired upon when Linderfelt the Butcher and his hell-hounds turned loose their machine guns and rifles upon the unprotected tented city of Ludlow, wiping it out of existence and killing men, women and children—mostly the latter.

The unionists had three American flags flying to the breeze on that bloody Monday.

But this made no difference to the gunmen who were wearing the state's uniforms.

Their deadly weapons tore the Stars and Stripes from their masts, just as if they had been so many rags.

They were burned when the torch was applied to the canvas homes.

It is a matter of general knowledge that the men under Chase, when they were sent into the field, never raised the American flag until they were in Ludlow several months.

Tuesday morning several undertakers went from Trinidad to the scene of the catastrophe, but were driven back by explosive bullets.

Railroad men and passengers appealed frantically to state officials to do something for the men, women and children who were lying along the railroad tracks dead and wounded.

For two days the bodies of Tikas and Fyler lay exposed. But no appeal would force the state officers to take care of the dead and wounded.

The fact that none of the bodies reported by railroad men could be found Wednesday, as well as the testimony of Mrs. Pearl Jolly, sometimes called the "heroine of Ludlow," explains this action.

Mrs. Jolly, with other women and children, escaped to a farm house late Monday afternoon. The next day, when the gunmen were looting the ruins of the tent colony, she says she saw them gathering bodies and placing them in a huge pile.

Dead Burned in Oil.

When they had completed their search, she says they poured oil on them and then burned the bodies. There are more than fifty women and children missing and it is believed that all traces of their murder were obliterated by the militia on the huge funeral pyre.

Mrs. Jolly during the battle went here and there through the tent colony, rescuing women and children and aiding the sick and wounded. Although she wore a Red Cross insignia on her arm, the uniformed gunmen tried to kill· her, one bullet tearing off the heel of her shoe.

John R. Lawson, National Board member of the mine workers, went to Ludlow Monday and Tuesday to save the women and children, and the militia riddled his flag of truce and drove him back.

William Snyder was coming from the tent colony Tuesday morning with his family, the body of his dead son on one arm and his baby daughter in the other, when he was discovered by some of the gunmen. One of the gunmen pointed a gun at him and said, "——— you, I have a notion to kill you, too."

Dave Stuart, a young boy, spent Monday and Monday night in the cellar of the Snodgrass store. When he went to the depot to go to Trinidad, he was lined up with other boys, from ten to twelve years of age, and told that the gunmen militia were going to use them for target practice.

Ludlow that morning presented a deep contrast to the day before.

Where for seven months 1,200 strikers had lived in peace, had subsisted on as little as possible, and had been happy in the realization that the dawn of a new day was at hand, now stood the charred ruins of their homes.

Where the day before 300 children had romped and played and had been happy now lay the distorted, roasted bodies of some of them and their mothers.

Louis Tikas, than whom there was none among the strikers more beloved, lay battered and dead along the railroad track, while the day before he had been visiting each tent, adding cheer to the men and their wives, trudging along with three or four children hanging to him, each one of them wanting him to come and help play their own particular game.

There lay the ruins of the Ludlow tent colony, the largest in the history of the world, and none knew or ever will know how many of its family of 1,200 paid the penalty of fighting for their constitutional rights in corporation-ridden Colorado.

Trinidad men who went to repair the telephone lines, cut by the murderers that the outside world might not know of their work of carnage, told one of the many pitiful stories of the massacre.

Tuesday they started toward Ludlow to repair the wires. They were going along the road when they saw a little girl lying at the side of the roadway.

She was lying there with the side of her head badly burned. In one hand she clasped a doll while the other arm was held across her eyes.

Just as the linemen were about to pick up the little sufferer, one of the brutal, murdering gunmen of Linderfelt's command stepped up to the lineman and told him to leave the little girl where she was.

None know what became of the little tot. It is believed that she contributed to the blaze on the funeral pyre erected to John D. Rockefeller Jr., Sunday school teacher and philanthropist.

Thirty women and children who escaped to the Powell ranch were held prisoners there until Tuesday night. They had nothing to eat or drink and appealed frantically to Trinidad for relief. Appeals were sent to Major Hamrock "to have mercy, for God's sake." Acting Governor Fitzgarrald, who vies with Ammons for the honor of being the real spineless executive of Colorado, finally ordered Saloonkeeper Hamrock to release the women.

Relief automobiles started from Trinidad at about the same time several wagons left Aguilar to their assistance. When the wagon approached the house, Mrs. Pearl Jolly, wearing a Red Cross insignia on her arm, went to meet it. She was shot in the arm made prominent by the Red Cross band.

The women, however, made their escape after a forty-eight-hour siege.

Mrs. M. H. Thomas was another of the women who was shot at by the murderers. She, with other women and children, escaped to a nearby ranch, where most of them were forced to sleep in filthy stable stalls to evade the exploding bullets from machine guns and high-powered rifles. When they ran for shelter Mrs. Thomas was so close to death that a bullet clipped out a part of her hair, and around the feet of her two little children played the machine gun bullets.

A freight train that came down the track about noon Tuesday enabled this party of refugees to escape. Knowing that the train would be between the gunmen and her people, Mrs. Thomas ran to the well and told others to try to make their escape. The entire party got away, but it was only because of poor marksmanship on the part of the gunmen, who riddled the air about them with hundreds of bullets.

Realizing that they had been betrayed by the state of Colorado and that they could hope to secure no protection from its militia, union men sent out an official call to arms, asking workers of the state and country to arm themselves and be ready to march at any minute.

The Call to Arms.

The official call was as follows:

Denver, Colo., April 22, 1914.

Organize the men in your community in companies of volunteers to protect the workers of Colorado against the murder and cremation of men, women and children by armed assassins in the employ of coal corporations, serving under the guise of state militiamen.

Gather together for defensive purposes all arms and ammunition legally available. Send name of leader of your company and actual num-

LIEUTENANT (BUTCHER) K. E. LINDERFELT

Whose operators' imported assassins were responsible for many of the horrors of Ludlow. Linderfelt broke the stock of his gun over Louis Tikas' head and is held responsible for his and other murders.

ber of men enlisted at once by wire, phone or
mail, to W T. Hickey, Secretary of State Federation of Labor

Hold all companies subject to order.

People having arms to spare for these defensive measures are requested to furnish same
to local companies, and, where no company exists, send them to the State Federation of Labor.

The state is furnishing us no protection and
we must protect ourselves, our wives and children, from these murderous assassins. We seek
no quarrel with the state and we expect to break
no law; we intend to exercise our lawful right
as citizens, to defend our homes and our constitutional rights.

JOHN R. LAWSON, U. M W. A.
JOHN McLENNAN
E L. DOYLE
JOHN RAMSAY
W. T. HICKEY, Secy. State Fed. of Lab.
E. R. HOAGE
T. W. TAYLOR
CLARENCE MOOREHOUSE
ERNEST MILLS, Secy.-Treas. W. F of M.

Offers of armed assistance came from all over
the country, and the workers responded just as
readily and liberally with contributions to relieve
the suffering men, women and children who had been
made homeless and left without food or clothing
by the terrible massacre.

One of the best descriptions of the Ludlow massacre was given by Godfrey Irwin, a young electrical engineer, in an interview with a New York
World reporter, which appeared in that paper
May 5. Irwin was employed by the Electrical
Transportation and Railroad Company in Trinidad.
The interview as it appeared in the New York
World follows:

"On the day of the Ludlow battle a chum and myself left the house of the Rev. J. O. Ferris, the Episcopal minister with whom I boarded in Trinidad, for a long tramp through the hills. We walked fourteen miles, intending to take the Colorado & Southern Railway back to Trinidad from Ludlow station.

"We were going down a trail on the mountain side above the tent city at Ludlow when my chum pulled my sleeve and at the same instant we heard shooting. The militia were coming out of Hastings Canyon and firing as they came. We lay flat behind a rock and after a few minutes I raised my hat aloft on a stick. Instantly bullets came in our direction. One penetrated my hat. The militiamen must have been watching the hillside through glasses and thought my old hat betrayed the whereabouts of a sharpshooter of the miners.

Saw Tikas Murdered.

"Then came the killing of Louis Tikas, the Greek leader of the strikers. We saw the militiamen parley outside the tent city, and, a few minutes later, Tikas came out to meet them. We watched them talking. Suddenly an officer raised his rifle, gripping the barrel, and felled Tikas with the butt.

"Tikas fell face downward. As he lay there we saw the militiamen fall back. Then they aimed their rifles and deliberately fired them into the unconscious man's body. It was the first murder I had ever seen, for it was a murder and nothing less. Then the miners ran about in the tent colony and women and children scuttled for safety in the pits which afterward trapped them.

"We watched from our rock shelter while the militia dragged up their machine guns and poured a murderous fire into the arroyo from a height by Water Tank Hill above the Ludlow depot. Then came the firing of the tents.

"I am positive that by no possible chance could they have been set ablaze accidentally. The militiamen were thick about the northwest corner of the colony where the fire started and we could see distinctly from our lofty observation place what looked like a blazing torch waved in the midst of militia a few seconds before the general conflagration swept through the place. What followed everybody knows.

"Sickened by what we had seen, we took a freight back into Trinidad. The town buzzed with indignation. To explain in large part the sympathies of even the best people in the section with the miners, it must be said that there is good evidence that many of the so-called 'militiamen' are only gunmen and thugs wearing the uniform to give them a show of authority. They are the toughest lot I ever saw.

"No one can legally enlist in the Colorado state militia till he has been a year in the state, and many of the 'militiamen' admitted to me they had been drafted in by a Denver detective agency. Lieutenant Linderfelt boasted that he was 'going to lick the miners or wipe them off the earth.' In Trinidad the miners never gave any trouble It was not till the militia came into town that the trouble began"

One of the refugees who arrived in Trinidad told the following story of the catastrophe:

"Monday morning when the people of Ludlow and the tent colony first got up they noticed that the gunmen were riding up and down in great haste, but thought nothing more of it. The strikers were sitting around in the same peaceable manner as usual.

"About 8:40 o'clock four 'gunmen-melish' were seen to go up to the tent colony They were hunting for one of the strikers. Louis Tikas told them if they would get a sheriff and a warrant, all right, but otherwise they couldn't have the party they were looking for. They went away, and, about 9 o'clock, gunmen were seen riding from the direction of Berwind. They rode to the C. & S. bridge and planted four gatling guns so they were pointing at the colony from the south. About 9:10 o'clock there were three bombs of dynamite fired, then, immediately, open fire was made upon the tent colony The shots rained continuously from that on Linderfelt was in the Ludlow depot with twelve other

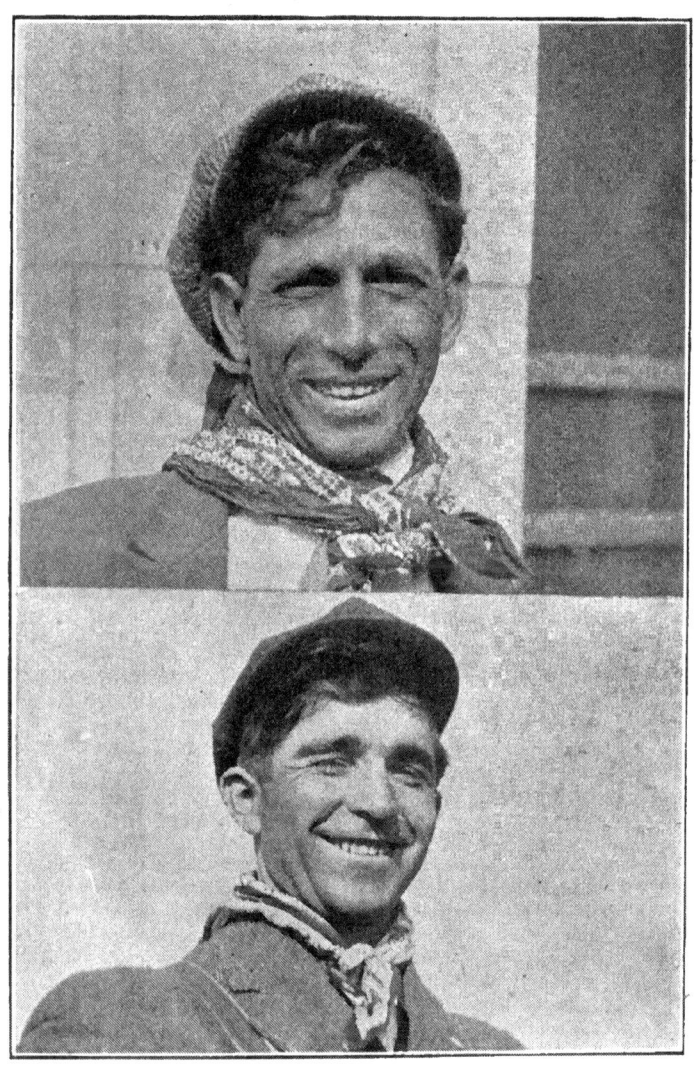

Above—"Little Pete," successor to Louis Tikas as leader of the Greeks.
Below—Amando Pelizarri, national organizer and leader of the Italians.

'braves,' and shot all day long from the depot
window. There were about 800 'scabs' with their
caps and candles on, directly out of the mine, who
were armed with Winchesters and made battle
upon the tent colony.

Threatened to Kill All.

"About 6 o'clock the door of the store was
battered in, the supplies were confiscated, and
then the store building was set fire to. From
that there were four other places within the tent
colony that were set fire. Linderfelt was heard
to remark, "There won't be a God-damned red-
neck left when we get through; we'll clean them
all." During the day he was asked how many
were killed. He said, "There are four of my
men killed and three injured; them Greeks are
damn crack shots. I went out with five men and
they shot three of them, one through the neck
and another through the shoulder.'

"Another gunmen leader was asked if there
was anyone left in the tents. He said, 'There
were four men in there, one of them sneaked
out to get some ammunition and I got him; then
two little girls came out all dressed in white.'
The other party said, 'You surely didn't shoot at
the little girls?' Gunman said, 'Your God damn
right I did.'

"When No. 2 Colorado & Southern train arrived from the north, they were still firing on
the colony. The tents were all ablaze. At the
time of the first shooting the women and children
had gone into the cellars where they would be
safe.

"As the tents burned, women and children
were seen to run out in the light of the blaze,
and just as fast as they came out they were shot
down. The gatling guns would rain bullets down
on them. There were six machine guns pelting
bullets all the time.

"The screams of the women and children
could be heard at the depot; they cried for
mercy, 'Oh, please don't kill us.' 'Oh, mamma,
what shall we do?' But they were shown no
mercy As they ran out in the glare of the fire,
bullets were rained on them, and then great yells

would go up from these depraved gunmen whose lust for blood even led them to kill women and babes. Every man who has any honor about him, every man all over the state and the nation should raise up in arms against this awful tyranny.

"One can hardly imagine such awfulness, and yet it happened, and strong men could hardly control their voice for emotion in talking of the awful deeds which were done in Ludlow today. One man said, 'If a little dog had been standing at Ludlow and witnessed the scene which took place there he must needs weep for the awfulness of it all.' "

John R. Lawson, active head of the strike at the time of the horror, bitterly denounced the gunmen militia:

Robbed the Dead.

"The hired assassins who are being paid $3 per day by the C. F. & I. and other companies for murdering innocent people do not understand that women and children are entitled to any respect or protection," said Lawson

"These beasts in human form have murdered these people by turning rapid-fire machine guns on the tent colony and with high-power rifles and explosive bullets, and, last but not least, they have robbed the dead and plundered the tents of the colony of everything of value and set the tent colony afire to obliterate as far as possible the bullet wounds on the dead and the tents that were filled with bullet holes.

"I have been informed that some of these Baldwin gunmen have even used dynamite to destroy the charred remains of innocent women and children, so that the world will never know the awful truth of the horrible murders.

"No one can fully realize the extent of this brutal outrage of shooting into the Ludlow tent colony in broad daylight and with the full knowledge that the tent colony contained many women and children and men who believed that they would be perfectly safe if they remained in their humble homes.

"It is unthinkable and unbelievable that there are fiends in human form that could be induced to commit these hellish acts. The cold-blooded murder of Louis Tikas does not come as a surprise to the people who knew him and his work, for Linderfelt and others in the Colorado National Guard said that they would kill him the first time they got a chance.

"John D. Rockefeller, Jr., may ease his conscience by attending Sunday school regularly in New York, but he will never be acquitted of committing the horrible atrocities that have occurred in a country such as America, and he will be convicted at the bar of public opinion for his part in the Colorado murders."

The report of the Women's Peace Association reveals some of the horrors of Ludlow, and, likewise, what representative women of the State of Colorado think of it. The report of the committee is all the more significant because of its personnel. None of these women are members of organized labor. They are in no way identified with the movement. The association is made up entirely of society and professional women.

The report is, in part, as follows:

May 7, 1914.

Hon. Elias M. Ammons, Governor:

Sir: The undersigned committee, appointed by the Women's Peace Association, and duly commissioned by you, has returned from Ludlow, and submits the following report:

Our investigations comprised interviews with militia officers and men, strike leaders and strikers, and with the District Attorney and various citizens of Las Animas County, and we beg to supplement this report with affidavits herewith attached.

Whatever feeling we may have had that accounts of the mine war had been exaggerated were soon dispelled. We declare to you that the half has not

Strike Breakers Capital Mine Lafayette Co

STRIKEBREAKERS

Compare the faces of these hired thugs with those of "Little Pete" and Pelizarri. Which do you think are the more desirable citizens and which would you prefer to have in your employ?

been told, and insist that any full and true relation
of actual events must expect to suffer by reason of
their very incredibility.

There is little use in recounting the details of
the Ludlow massacre. Suffice it to say that we place
the entire blame for this horror on the imported
assassins who masqueraded as sons of Colorado in
the uniform of the National Guard.

Massacre Deliberately Planned.

There is no question in our minds but that the
attack on the tent colony was planned with care and
executed in cold blood. No sooner was the main
body of the militia withdrawn from the strike district than a new company was hastily formed out
of the mine guards, mine employes, itinerant gunmen and slum sweepings. Known as Troop "A,"
this officerless, un-uniformed detachment, together
with the desperadoes under the command of Linderfelt in Company "B," formed the attacking force.

The three machine guns were planted in posi-
tion prior to Monday morning. We were unable to
discover that a single gun was fired prior to the
explosion of the three bombs that Major Hamrock
admitted to be his own signal for the battle to begin.
The utter unpreparedness of the strikers for fighting is demonstrated by the fact that many of the
women and children were still in bed, and were compelled to flee for their lives half dressed.

We also found that Major Hamrock tested the
range of his machine guns by firing into the first
line of tents, and that later in the engagement soldiers soaked paper in oil and used these torches to
spread the conflagration.

Wholesale looting followed the massacre, and
one of the pictures painted for us by homeless
women was that of the soldiers carrying trunks to
the station, dancing with stolen blankets about their
heads to the music of a stolen accordion, and grab-

bing here and there in the tents for valuables. In support of these assertions, we direct your attention specifically to the affidavits of Mrs. Pedregon, Mrs. Bertoloti and Mrs. Chavez, whose savings and household goods were taken, and to that of Mrs. Ed Tonner, which tells how a soldier lighted a broom soaked in oil and set fire to the tent in which she huddled with her five children.

Baby Born as Mother Flees.

Fifty of these hunted women, we beg to state, were about to become mothers, and one unfortunate actually gave birth to her baby while trying to escape the hail of bullets from Hamrock's machine guns. Many ran eight or ten miles in their mad terror, and others huddled in wells and holes for eighteen hours without food.

In many instances we are compelled to disagree absolutely with your military committee. Their report states that the Greeks ruled the colony, while we assert that no nationality had a dominant voice —the twenty-six races living and acting in a spirit of fraternity remarkable to behold. That Louis Tikas was the recognized leader of the colony was not due to the fact of his being a Greek, but to his ability and the love and confidence he inspired. At this point, we cannot too strongly condemn the circumstances of his death. No doubt remains in our minds that Tikas and Fyler, the two leaders, were murdered while in the custody of soldiers, and that the Greek was deliberately clubbed by Lieutenant Linderfelt while standing helpless and unarmed. Not in the annals of civilized warfare is there record of anything more inhuman than the cold-blooded killing of these two prisoners.

We must also disagree with the military committee in the matter of the death of Frankie Snyder. According to the report, the father of the boy told them that Frankie was killed while facing the ar-

royo, meaning that the strikers had shot him; also
that the elder Snyder told them that the Greeks
planned the battle in advance, and that they were
to blame for the entire trouble.

Talking face to face with us, and signing an
affidavit, Snyder declared that Frankie had been
shot down by the soldiers while cradling his little
sister in his arms. He also charged the militia with
firing the first shot, insisting that the attack was
unexpected, and his bitterness was extreme in tell-
ing how the militia dashed into the tent where the
dead boy lay and called the weeping mother un-
printable names.

We cannot believe that Snyder ever told the
military committee any such tale as they print, and,
if he did so, it must have been under the same com-
pulsion that induced one striker to dig what he
thought to be his own grave.

Brutal Officers Condemned.

We disagree also with the brutal and contemp-
tuous language in which Messrs. Boughton, Danks
and Van Cise dismiss the strikers as "ignorant, lawless and savage South European peasants." This
is the judgment of men who have never known what
it is to work, whose activities are entirely parasitic,
and who have no other standard of comparison than
the rich and the idle

We declare to you that the Ludlow tent colony,
from what we learned, was a community of decent
people, passionately proud of their little tents, domestic to the last degree, generous and loving in
their dealings with one another, and, altogether,
evincing in every relation of life a brotherhood that
shames many a Christian American.

There is no question in our minds that Colorado
has in them the making of a virile, intelligent citizenship, and it is in this connection that we want to
point out to you how absolutely the state has failed

in its duty to these foreigners who have been brought into our midst for assimilation.

There is no question that the coal companies have violated every law on the statute books for the protection of their employes. From the commencement of their residence in this land of the free, these people from other lands have been made the victims of unbearable oppressions. Herded like cattle, cheated on the weight of coal they produced, the victims of extortion at every turn, and unprotected by proper safety appliances and improvements, they were given small conception of the justice that is the keystone in our national arch. Their sole contact with the spirit of citizenship was during elections, when they were driven to the polls by superintendents and voted like sheep.

Nor when the militia came into the district, at your command, was the situation bettered in the slightest degree. We talked with any number of women who told us that they welcomed the soldiery at first, feeling that they came to restore peace and promote justice. But when they saw among the troops the very mine guards, detectives and gunmen that had been persecuting them, and when these men commenced to beat, insult, abuse and arrest them, their welcome turned to hatred.

Flag Trampled in Dust.

Even the children are imbibing a spirit of hatred and bitterness that will be detrimental to their growth as desirable citizens. We insist that these foreigners learn to love the flag, yet, when the union women of Trinidad took $300 of their saved pennies and bought the Stars and Stripes to fly over a parade, they were ridden down by the soldiery, and the national colors trampled in the dust. Women and children were given sabre scars that they will carry to the grave; a 16-year-old girl was kicked in the breast by the commanding officer, and others were maimed by having gun butts dropped on their feet.

We could wish to have pages to recite the tortures and injustices to which the men, women and children of the strikers were subjected. Many were arrested without warrant or apparent reason, thrown into jail and actually forgotten as far as any hearing was concerned. The following case may be cited as typical.

Mrs. Mary M. Thomas, a frail little Welsh woman, and the mother of two little children, was arrested on the streets of Trinidad, subjected to abuse and insult, and confined for three weeks in a vermin-ridden cell. Food was thrown to her as though she had been a beast. Her letters of appeal went unanswered, and she was released at last without one word of explanation or apology.

It is hardly necessary to recount the experiences of "Mother" Jones. Regardless of what one may think of her opinions or her utterances, surely humanity must sicken at the imprisonment of this old woman of 82 in a rat-infested basement, held on no charge whatever, and denied the right to see friends or counsel, and all this time guarded by four stalwart troopers.

Try as we could, we failed to find that the coal companies had the slightest conception of their duty to these aliens for whose presence in the state they are solely responsible. Out of their vicious insistence upon profits alone, they disregarded the fact that these people and their children constituted a problem in citizenship that must be solved if our social structure is to endure. They have taught hate and violence, prevented understanding and education, all to the result that the people of Colorado are now confronting a danger that can only be averted by our utmost justice and wisest statesmanship.

We are glad, indeed, to be able to report that

ARMED STRIKERS IN CAMP AT SAN RAFAEL HEIGHTS, TRINIDAD, COLO.

San Rafael Hospital, where Mother Jones was held incommunicado by the militia for nine weeks, can be seen in the distance.

the real Sons of Colorado in the militia seem to
have played small part in this reign of terror. The
brutalities complained of were inflicted almost entirely by the mine guards and hired thugs rushed
into the militia by the coal companies, many of them
still remaining on the company pay-rolls.

The attitude of these creatures was not the
least repulsive features of our investigation. Many
of those with whom we talked actually viewed the
Ludlow massacre as "fun."

In view of all these things, we beg to make the
following recommendations:

1.   That you order an instant investigation of
all happenings connected with the presence of the
militia in the strike district, to the end that a distinction may be established between rightful exer-
cises of the military power and the crimes of individuals, turning latter cases over to the civil authorities for prompt prosecution. The eyes of the
world are upon us, and the honor of Colorado demands that the state refuse to bear the odium of
atrocities committed by imported Hessians.

2.   That the extra session make no provision
for the payment of the indebtedness incurred by the
militia until the military rolls have been purged of
the Rockefeller gunmen and thugs, and until an
auditing committee has made a report that will per-
mit the people to decide between just obligations
and fraudulent claims. It is the right of Colorado
to have a distinction established between the bona
fide, law-loving members of our national guard and
the desperadoes sneaked into it by the companies.

3.   That you withdraw your request for a state
constabulary, as such an organization could not help
becoming a powerful adjunct to the labor-crushing
despotism of the coal companies.

4.   That you exercise your police power and
take over the mines for operation by the state, pending an agreement between the strikers and the oper-

ators. Had this been done in the first place, Colorado would not now be burdened with debt and unmerited shame.

5. That you lend your aid to the movement in favor of a constitutional amendment allowing the state to develop its own natural resources, so that we may be freed from the menace of such absentee landlords as Rockefeller, whose only interest in our affairs is the money that his overseers may mint from the sweat of wage-slaves.

It is our opinion, sir, that the time has come for some enunciation of the great truth that the rights of society are paramount, and that no individual, group, corporation or class shall be permitted to advance its own interests at the expense of the general welfare. Strikes and lockouts are alike antagonistic to public peace and prosperity.

The public must stretch out its hand, still all strife and adjust disputes in the spirit of *equal justice* that takes no account of *race, circumstances* or *creed*. The people—third party to every industrial dispute—must assert their incontrovertible claim to act as arbiter.

President Wilson expects you "to draw the attention of the Legislature to the imperative necessity of immediate consideration of the whole situation and secure as prompt action as is possible in the premises."

What will you do?

Respectfully submitted,
ALMA V. LAFFERTY,
EVANGELINE HEARTZ,
Committee.

Affidavits of Survivors of the Massacre Tell the Terrible Story

State of Colorado, ' } ss.   AFFIDAVIT
County of Las Animas }

Tom Romero, being first duly sworn, upon oath doth depose and say:

That his name is Tom Romero; that on Monday, April 20th, about 9 a. m., he was playing ball back of the Snodgrass store at Ludlow with one Frank Didano; that he heard some explosions and saw some men and women running from the depot at Ludlow toward the tent colony; that he saw some soldiers and guards near the steel bridge and some more over near the soldiers' camp, working with a machine gun; that he and Frank Didano ran for the tent colony; that right away machine guns opened fire on the tent colony, and the people hid in the cellars of the tents to keep from getting killed and some ran for the arroyo; that affiant ran for the arroyo and took with him some women and children whom he persuaded to run the risk of the machine guns; that some people got killed running from the tents to the arroyo and other places; that the firing got so hot that no one dared to try to get back to the tents; several men had tried it and got killed; they got more machine guns and put them on a hill so they could shoot down in the arroyo, and affiant then ran away and came to Trinidad; that affiant had no gun; that there were not over fifty guns in the tent colony that affiant knows of, including shotguns; that no shooting was done by anyone from the tent colony; that they tried to kill every living thing with their machine guns.

(Signed)   TOM ROMERO.

Subscribed in my presence and sworn to before me this 23rd day of April, A. D. 1914.

My commission expires on the 18th day of July, A. D. 1915.

(Seal)   ANGUS E. McGLASHAN,
                        Notary Public.

THE "BLACK HOLE" OF LUDLOW

State of Colorado, } ss.   AFFIDAVIT
County of Las Animas {

John Boga, of lawful age, being first duly sworn, upon oath doth depose and say:

That his name is John Boga; that he is a striking miner; that on Monday, April 20th, he was in the tent colony; that the tent colony had many American flags on flagstaffs over the tents, as well as other flags; that about 9 o'clock he heard an explosion that sounded like a cannon or dynamite over near the soldiers' tent, and affiant ran out of his tent and immediately the soldiers and guards started shooting into the tent colony; that affiant had no gun, and ran for his life into the arroyo and stayed there until about 2 o'clock in the afternoon, when he saw an automobile on the road being shot at by a machine gun, and affiant ran out and found it was John Lawson trying to get to the tent colony, and rode back with him to Hoehne and then came to Trinidad; that there was no shooting done by anyone from the tent colony ground; the few men who had guns went away to other places, and there was no excuse to shoot into the tents.

. (Signed)   JOHN BOGA.

Subscribed in my presence and sworn to before me this 23rd day of April, A. D. 1914.

My commission expires on the 18th day of July, A. D. 1915.

(Seal)   ANGUS E. McGLASHAN,
                         Notary Public.

State of Colorado, } ss   AFFIDAVIT
County of Las Animas {

John Oleko, of lawful age, being first duly sworn, upon oath doth depose and say:

That his name is John Oleko; that he is a resident of the Ludlow tent colony; that he is of Slavish nationality; that he went to the store at Ludlow, which is about 200 yards from the tent colony, on Monday morning, April 20, A. D. 1914, to buy some things from the store; that about 9 o'clock he came back to his tent, which is No. 120, and in a moment or two he heard a big shot over near the soldiers' camp; he came out of his tent and heard another big shot; pretty soon shooting from soldiers' camp and from all over that way started by men shooting toward the tent colony; affiant got scared and tried to get some Slavish women and children to leave the tents and hide in the arroyo or run away; that affiant had no gun and there were very few guns in the tents; that he did succeed in getting three women and several children down in the creek, but was all the time shot at by rifles and machine guns; that the soldiers and guards shoot thousands and thousands of shots through the tents; that men who try to go get women out of tent get killed; that they holler for women to come down in the creek, but they were afraid, and affiant thinks that they would all have been killed had they tried to cross the open space from the tents to the arroyo; if the tents had not been burned, the women and children who had hid in the holes under the tents might have been all right, unless the explosive bullets hit near them; affiant could not do anything, so he ran away to a ranch and came to Trinidad, where he has been since.

(Signed) JOHN OLEKO.

Subscribed in my presence and sworn to before me this 23rd day of April, A. D. 1914.

My commission expires on the 18th day of July, A. D. 1915.

(Seal) ANGUS E. McGLASHAN,
Notary Public.

Military Report

A military committee composed of Judge Advocate Boughton of the notorious military court, Captain W. C. Danks and Captain Philip Van Cise did not deny in its report that the tent colony had been fired and looted by the thugs after the massacre of the innocents. The report says:

"During the rescuing, and afterwards, the tent colony was invaded by the soldiers and mine guards for quite a different purpose. By this time the uniformed guardsmen had been joined by large numbers of men in civilian attire, part of whom were from Troop "A" and part of them mine guards, all unknown to the uniformed soldiers and their officers and all unused and unamenable to discipline.

"By this time, the time of the burning of the tents, the nondescript number of men had passed out of their officers' control, had ceased to be an army and had become a mob. Doubtless all were seeing red on both sides of the conflict.

"We find that the tents were not all of them destroyed by accidental fire. Men and soldiers swarmed into the colony and deliberately assisted the conflagration of spreading the fire from tent to tent.

"Beyond a doubt, it was seen to intentionally that the fire should destroy the whole of the colony. This, too, was accompanied by the usual loot.

"Men and soldiers seized and took from the tents whatever appealed to their fancy of the moment. In this way, clothes, bedding, articles of jewelry, bicycles, tools and utensils were taken from the tents and conveyed away.

"So deliberate was this burning and looting that we find that cans of oil found in the tents were poured upon them and the tents lit with matches."

LOUIS TIKAS
Murdered Hero

This photograph of Louis, the Greek, was taken at
the well of the Ludlow tent colony several months before the disaster. It illustrates the extremes to which the
state militia went to harass the strikers—one of Linderfelt's murderers fell from his horse when the animal
stumbled over a piece of wire. Linderfelt ordered all the
wire fence around the tent colony cut down. It was
thrown into the only well from which the strikers could
get water. Louis is standing beside the wire and a pole
after they were taken from the well.

This committee did not hesitate to fix the blame and to say that the battle was premeditated and deliberately planned.

The report says:

"We find that the remote cause of this, as of all other battles, lies with the coal operators who established in an American industrial community a numerous class of ignorant, lawless and savage South European peasants. The present underlying cause was the presence near Ludlow, in daily contact one with another, of three discordant elements—strikers, soldiers and mine guards, all armed and fostering an increasing deadly hatred which sooner or later was bound to find some such expression"

But the scenes at Ludlow were none the less pathetic than those in Trinidad, where several hundred women and children found refuge. Society women, who had been openly opposed to the miners, offered their homes to the survivors of the horrible massacre with the same spirit as the working people offered to share their two and three rooms.

In the halls of the Trinidad Trades and Labor Assembly most of the refugees were housed. No pen could picture the scenes of suffering or anguish portrayed there.

Whole Families Wiped Out.

Over in one corner was Mrs Mary Petrucci, driven temporarily insane over the loss of her three little children.

Not far away sat Piedro Valdez, his short, stocky frame shaking in agonized grief over the terrible extermination of his entire family.

Piedro was in El Paso when he heard that the battle had started. He thought of his brother and his wife and four children who were in the tent colony, and left at once for Trinidad. When he reached there, Tuesday, he found his brother dead

PROCESSION OF STRIKERS AT THE FUNERAL OF LOUIS TIKAS IN TRINIDAD

from an explosive bullet and his wife and four children burned and emaciated so terribly that they could scarcely be recognized.

From every corner of the immense hall came wails and sobs for loved ones known to be dead or missing.

It was not until Wednesday, forty-eight hours after the massacre of the innocents at Ludlow, that the militia allowed Red Cross nurses and physicians to go to the scene of the disaster. Then they were not allowed to search the ruins.

In one cave alone, the "Black Hole of Ludlow," were found the emaciated bodies of eleven little children, none of whom were over seven years of age, and two of their mothers.

Their faces, drawn taut with pain, showed the terrible torture they had suffered before death, and their burned bodies put the lie to the militia's story that they had been suffocated.

Flames Cheat Bullets.

One of these little tots who had been hiding in a tent tried to escape when the gunmen militia set fire to the tent colony Monday night. She was driven back into the flaming furnace by the assassins' bullets and burned to death.

It is believed that many of the children met their deaths in the same manner. It would have been impossible for the thirteen women and children found in the "Black Hole" to have been burned there.

Some of those found dead there were not burned. These were the children who were taken to this place of safety by Louis Tikas and others before the colony was destroyed.

The others were probably picked up in the various tents and thrown into the hole to create the impression that no women and children were murdered and cremated by the militiamen, but that all of those found were suffocated in caves dug for their safety by their fathers and husbands.

President John McLennan of District 15, one of the active leaders of the strike, went with the Red Cross party to Ludlow. He had been given permission to go there, but as soon as he arrived he was placed under arrest. He was released, but had only been at liberty a few minutes when he was again taken into custody and held until the party was ready to leave.

The fact that the Red Cross party and undertakers were not allowed to search the ruins, and that President McLennan was not even permitted to go over the ground seems to further prove the claim that only a small percentage of the murdered were found and that the gunmen militia had even more than that to hide from strike officials and the public.

The bodies of the dead were taken to the Hall-McMahon undertaking parlors in Trinidad.

And for the next forty-eight hours weeping and wailing men and women crowded the place, hoping against hope that they would find none of their loved ones there, and yet seeming to wish that they would rather have them dead than among the missing who might never return from the scene of the slaughter.

Death Beats Life.

Death, represented by the Hamrock-Linderfelt butchers, beat Life in the struggle, and young strikers were the penalty. They were just some of the many cases where the innocent had to suffer.

One particular instance of the results of this butchery was had in the undertaking parlor that night.

The young striker was unarmed.

Its mother lay on a cold, hard slab at the morgue, a victim of the Hamrock-Linderfelt murderers. She was found in the death hole at Ludlow when the Red Cross Society visited the devastated city.

If the murderous thugs in Colorado's national guard uniform had remained away from Ludlow, had not felt it necessary to massacre the innocents to earn their $3 additional pay from the coal operators, there would have been at least one little striker two days old. But the Hamrock-Linderfelt assassins' lust for blood could not be denied.

Thursday morning when the woman was buried a little heap lay in her arms against a breast that never had or never would nurse it.

Trinidad turned out *en masse* to do honor to the massacred dead when they were buried.

The wails and chants of the women who were mourning their dead caused tears of sympathy to flow from eyes that had formerly looked askance at these same people.

As they passed the coffins of these poor dead little children, charred and reddened by the fire, their features distorted by the agony in which they died, the heart-cries of the mourners swelled into a monster voice of protest against the terrible outrage.

Many of the women and children were in such a horribly mutilated condition that the caskets were closed.

There were none who watched this funeral procession who did not think of the words of the Risen God as He said: "For it is written vengeance is mine, I will repay saith the Lord."

Louis the Greek was buried in the Knights of Pythias cemetery on Monday, one week after he had made himself a martyr to the cause of his union and his people, whom he rescued by the score.

To show the fellowship of the dead man for his comrades at Ludlow, the body of Tikas, in a flower-covered casket, had headed the funeral procession of those who had been buried the Thursday before.

STRIKING COAL MINERS' TENT COLONY AT LUDLOW, COLORADO,

Before it was destroyed and nineteen of its inhabitants murdered and cremated by Colorado gunmen-militia, April 20, 1914.

NEAR VIEW OF RUINS OF LUDLOW TENT COLONY

Then the body was returned to the undertaking parlors to await the arrival of a priest of the Greek Catholic Church.

All day Sunday hundreds of strikers, hats in hand, had marched past the bier of Tikas. They solemnly touched the cold brow, crossed themselves, muttered something and then quickened their steps for the strikers' camp at San Rafael Heights.

Funeral of Louis Tikas.

Frances Wayne described Louis' funeral as follows:

"The body of Tikas lay before an altar on which were branched candles, holding high, burning tapers. The priest, assisted by Pietro Catsulis, now the leader of the Greek colony, intoned the mass, the response being made by Catsulis.

"Three times the priest kissed the cheeks of the dead leader. Three times he anointed the brow with wine. Three times he sprinkled dust on the face of the dead, while a Greek in overalls and corduroy coat swung the silver censer and wailed dolefully.

" 'Jesus give a place in Heaven to Louis,' chanted the priest in the Greek tongue.

" 'Jesus give a place in heaven to Louis. Bring life from the grave,' solemnly repeated the darkfaced fighting men who crowded the undertaker's chapel.

" 'Jesus, if Louis has any enemies, may they forget their hostility,' chanted Catsulis.

"The tapers burned low. The place was dim with incense. But the priest chanted on, his irongray hair and flowing beard in somber contrast with his gold and silver woven robes.

"This was the funeral of the man beliked by all he led and served. But a handful of women were present, and no arms were carried to remind those who watched that war was on.

"Orderly, reverent, deeply religious, was the service. When the body was carried from the chapel, 488 Greeks followed the line before the hearse. The American colors, draped in crepe, were lifted, and in utter silence the cortege moved down Main Street to Commercial, past the headquarters of the United Mine Workers and on over the hill to the Knights of Pythias cemetery.

"Before the funeral four Greeks carrying their muskets entered the chapel. They lifted their hats, muttered an oath to 'avenge Louis' death,' pounded four times on the floor with their muskets, turned and left the room."

The "Ludlow Massacre" started a two weeks' war between strikers and gunmen that has probably never been equalled for its viciousness in any industrial conflict.

Attempt Wholesale Slaughter.

Driven frantic and more bloodthirsty by the cries of protest that came from all parts of the world against their infamous slaughter of the women and children at Ludlow, the gunmen militia started what they hoped would be the complete extermination of the strikers and their families.

President McLennan was arrested Thursday by the militia and held all night. Every few minutes his life was threatened, but he was finally released.

While Red Cross nurses waited in his office to get permits to aid the injured at Ludlow, Acting Governor Fitzgarrald held an hour's conference with the coal operators Tuesday afternoon. The result of that conference was an order returning the militia to the field the following day to reinforce the murderers of Saloonkeeper Hamrock and Butcher Linderfelt.

The Trinidad Free Press fixed the blame for sending out the militia as follows:

"Orders to acting Governor Fitzgarrald to send

gunmen reinforcements to the strike zone to back
up the gunmen who massacred the women and children at Ludlow Monday were carried direct from
the office of John C. Osgood, president of the Victor-
American Fuel Co., to the state capitol Wednesday
morning by President Stearns of the Chamber of
Commerce and Fred P. Johnson, political agent of
the Chicago packing trust.

"Assurances of ample funds for the campaign
were also taken to Fitzgarrald by those active agents
of Rockefellers and other special privilege interests.

"And Fitzgarrald lost no time in conveying the
coal operators' orders to Chase.

"Chase was delighted.

"He immediately began notifying Denver militiamen, whose mothers and wives were raging
against the Ludlow massacre, to hold themselves in
readiness to entrain for the strike zone.

"Fitzgarrald, alarmed at the protest of Demo-
cratic leaders over his refusal to go in person to
Ludlow and stop the fighting, feared that the fact
he was carrying out the Ammons policy of doing the
coal barons' bidding, gave out an interview Thursday night saying he had refused the operators' offer
of money to finance the state troops.

"Stearns was ordered to come to Osgood's office
in the E. & C. building. A few minutes later, Johnson arrived. Other visitors were swept aside. A
hurried conference followed.

"Then the orders were taken to Fitzgarrald. He
immediately told Chase to get in touch with his men.
Telegrams were sent to Governor Ammons, who was
en route home from Washington, where he had been
lobbying for land grabbers, who want further li-
cense to loot public lands in Colorado.

"Thus was Fitzgarrald lending his ear to the
coal barons and obeying their orders Wednesday,
while the Ludlow murderers were driving away undertakers sent from Trinidad to Ludlow to recover

the burned and mangled forms of those little children
and brave women who died by fire and bullet.

Horror Shocks Colorado.

Colorado stood aghast at the horrors of the
shambles of Ludlow.

Persons who had been prostituted to favor the
militia before this catastrophe bowed their heads
and apologized that they were residents of a state
where its alleged citizen soldiery should be used to
murder the working class and its women and babes.

Men and women stood on the streets talking in
a whisper of this horror.

Organizations passed resolutions, some offering
armed assistance to the strikers and asking to be
called.

Many bodies turned over their entire treasuries
to aid the suffering men and women and children.

More than 1,000 women—many carrying babes
in their arms—stormed the capitol Saturday at the
call of the Women's Peace organization and ordered
Governor Ammons to ask President Wilson to send
federal troops to end the civil war which flamed red
in the strike zone following the "Slaughter of Innocents" at Ludlow Monday by Rockefeller gunmen
wearing militia uniforms.

They sang "America" and other patriotic songs
while Ammons waited for detectives to escort him
into the presence of outraged maidens, wives and
mothers, who were so aroused over the massacre
of defenseless women and innocent children at Ludlow.

Ammons tried to refuse their plea for an immediate request for federal troops.

"Punish those guilty of the Ludlow massacre,"
was the battle cry as the women gathered.

"Wait until I investigate and get the facts,"
he pleaded. "It would be an AFFRONT TO PRES-

President John McLennan of District 15, U. M. W. A., and Major Pat Hamrock, saloon-keeper and officer in charge of Colorado's uniformed murderers who perpetrated the Ludlow Massacre.

Picture taken when McLennan was a military prisoner.

IDENT WILSON TO ASK FOR FEDERAL
TROOPS NOW.''

"May I respectfully ask in what way it would
be an affront to ask the president for help when he
has said he was willing to help if you will ask for
troops?" said Mrs. Robert W. Steele, widow of Chief
Justice R. W. Steele, who led the delegation of men,
women and children.

Waiting hundreds cheered when the brave little
widow of the clear visioned late supreme court justice challenged the governor.

Ammons refused to answer this question. He
talked all around the point, but Colorado mothers
do not yet understand how it is an affront to demand
the stopping of civil war on women and children.

A thunderous cry for immediate action by the
governor in telegraphing to Washington for troops
forced him to promise the women that he would send
a message at once to find whether or not he could
have federal troops if he asked for them.

He was escorted to his office by the same committee of women which demanded his presence in
the house.

A telegram from Representative Taylor of Colorado had announced that federal troops could not be
sent even if asked for since there was no precedent
for such action by federal authorities.

Wilson was ready to send troops if Governor
Ammons would ask for them.

These conflicting statements caused the message
of inquiry to be sent.

Senator Helen Ring Robinson, Mrs. S. K. Wall-
ing, Mrs. Evangeline Heartz, Mrs. J. J. Ryan and
Mrs. J. C. Herrlingger, carrying her eight-months-
old baby, camped in Governor Ammons' office for an
hour before he would go to the house chamber to
get his answer from Washington.

Governor Ammons publicly promised the women

that he would find the guilty and PUNISH them for the Ludlow massacre.

He said there had been constant firing in the southern coal fields since 6 a. m. and he had been trying to stop the battles between strikers and state militia.

This is the telegram Ammons sent:

"To the President,
    "White House,
        "Washington, D. C.

"Conflicting reports as to action at cabinet meeting yesterday morning have been received here. I would be greatly obliged to know if we cannot control the situation in the southern coal fields, can we have federal troops?
                    "ELIAS AMMONS."

After reading this message, to which no answer had yet been received, the assembly was dismissed, with a large delegation remaining to get the answer when it is received.

The women were waiting in the house chamber for the president's answer to Ammons' wire for federal troops. The women did not leave for lunch. When leaders suggested that a large committee be named to relieve the meeting from the duty of waiting, cries of "No, no," came from the audience.

Company Doctors Kill Babes.

During the speechmaking while the women waited for Ammons to put in an appearance, another kind of "slaughter of innocents" was described by Mrs. Mary L. Geffs, 5025 Tennyson street, who went personally into the southern coal fields to investigate conditions.

"And what of the coal company doctors," she cried in a ringing voice.

"Let me tell you how babes are killed by willful neglect of camp doctors who pretended to care for the women at confinement.

"I know personally of many babies born to miners' wives who died through the carelessness of a corporation-hired doctor to whom every mother paid tribute of $1 a month. Oh, sisters, let me tell you a coal miner's wife has just as much love for her child as you have for yours.

"I believe they have even more devotion to their babes than the rich, whom I have heard divide their affection between their children and their poodle dogs. Do you realize that this sort of child murder has been going on for twenty-five years in our coal camps?

"When the camp doctor was refused by some wives and another physician brought in to care for them, he WAS CHASED OUT OF THE CAMP by coal company guards.

"Women, hear me when I tell you these are facts gathered by a woman who does not live in southern Colorado, who is not a miner's wife and who went there unbiased to learn the truth."

These women camped in the state house until Ammons finally granted their demand and asked President Wilson to send federal troops to Colorado.

The people of Colorado found one outlet for their bitter feeling of protest against the slaughter of the innocents in a monster mass meeting held on the state house grounds in Denver Sunday afternoon, April 26.

Prominent citizens of Denver got together and issued the following call for the meeting:

Ludlow—A Call to Action

A mass meeting will be held Sunday afternoon on the State House grounds at 3 o'clock to take action upon the Ludlow massacre. All those to whom patriotism means more than profits, and in whom humanity still burns, are urged to attend and breathe their passion into the dead body of murdered justice. Betrayed by those elected to protect, and butchered by brutal mercenaries, the only hope of the toiling class now lies in common counsel and concerted action. Desperate is the need. The money masters, realizing that we will not surrender as long as life lasts, are resolved upon a campaign of utter annihilation. Of all those who labor, whether in mine, mill, shop or store, not one is safe from capitalism's savage menace. It is the turn of the miners today. Oh, brothers in other callings, it may be yours tomorrow. It is not a handful of coal diggers that have been marked down for slaughter; it is the right of the worker to better his condition that they mean to destroy. If Ludlow shall go unanswered it will be the death knell of human hope and human aspiration. Let the blood of those martyred men, women and babes wash away all lines of difference and division, permitting brotherhood to stand forth free again and whole. Come.

WORKERS' DEFENSE LEAGUE.

Ten thousand men and women stood in a driving rain for two hours that Sunday afternoon and listened to stirring denunciations of the gunmen-militiamen by Mother Jones, E L. Doyle, secretary-treasurer of District 15 of the United Mine Workers, and others.

Resolutions of Meeting.

There in front of the state capitol, where Colorado officials had betrayed its citizens, the following resolutions were passed:

To All the People:

This meeting gathered under the open skies, cries to the world the record of industrial wrongs that found ghastly culmination in the wanton massacre of men, women and children under the burning tents at Ludlow.

There are laws upon the statute books of Colorado that guarantee to miners the eight-hour day, cash payment for work, semi-monthly pay-days, the right to unionization, check weighmen and the protection of safety devices.

Absentee landlords operating on land stolen from the school children of Colorado, their humanity stifled by avarice, have defied every one of these laws continuously and openly. More than 2,000 miners have died like rats in traps these last twenty years because dividends could not be lessened by the expense of improvements, and their families denied the right to collect damages have been doomed to squalor and despair.

This cruel control has been obtained by the purchase of state, county and municipal officials, seizure of the election machinery, the peonage of employes, the use of hired desperadoes and the constant threat of the state militia, all to the end that justice has been crushed and a sovereign state buried in shame and disaster.

Revolt has come at last. Twelve thousand wretched men, speaking thirty-six different tongues, have found common voice in a cry of despair that shakes the world. It is to their relief that we dedicate our lives and our liberties.

We demand the instant seizure of the coal mines by the state pending an agreement between the operators and the strikers.

We demand that the leases of 13,276 acres of school land, for which the companies pay a beggarly rental, be cancelled at once, and plans laid instantly

The Militia Made Andrew Colnar Dig His Own Grave

for development by the state of the 473,000 acres of coal land owned by the state.

We demand a constitutional amendment repealing the infamous Moyer decision rendered by corrupt judges to rob the humble and oppressed of their most sacred constitutional guarantees.

We demand that our legislature repudiate the $1,000,000 debt that the coal companies' use of the militia has saddled upon the state, thereby forcing capital to pay its own bills.

Governor a Traitor.

We brand Elias M. Ammons, governor, and S. R. Fitzgarrald, lieutenant governor, as traitors to the people and accessories to the murder of babies, and we call upon the special session of the legislature to impeach them as false to their oaths and their God, and if there be no special session, we hereby pledge ourselves to institute recall proceedings so that these servile tools of special privilege may be deprived of their power to betray and oppress.

And, lest it be thought that these are but hasty determinations that will pass with the passion of the moment, we call upon the justice-loving citizens of Colorado to arm themselves so that if law and order be still defied, we may be able to protect our homes, our loved ones and our sacred rights.

Mutiny in Militia.

Six hundred men were ordered out by Czar Chase. But the Ludlow massacre was even a stench in the nostrils of some of the militiamen who had previously terrorized the strike district by robberies and outrages of women and children, and only about 350 state troopers went to the field.

With the aid of operators' machine guns and state equipment, they left nothing undone to destroy the miners and their families. For six months they had been in the field in an effort to break the strike and had failed.

The Ludlow horror was planned and carried out in the belief that this massacre of women and children would certainly break the spirit of the striking miners. But even this terrible holocaust would not stop the miners from fighting for their rights.

So now came the state's militia back to the field to attempt a complete physical extermination of the strikers.

In every section of Las Animas, Huerfano and Fremont counties Colorado's representative troopers joined the murderous mine guards in attacks upon the miners.

In Boulder county where the northern strike has been fought for four years, the Baldwin-Feltz detectives and mine guards started to do the work alone.

Machine guns were turned on the towns of Lafayette and Louisville in an attempt to slaughter the strikers and their families who make up the greater part of the population of these towns.

Women and children were driven from their homes to Denver, where they were taken care of at hotels by the United Mine Workers. For five days the militia and imported gunmen waged this war upon the union coal miners.

Strikers Repel Murderers.

But Ludlow had taught the strikers a lesson. They were prepared against a possible repetition of the Ludlow horror. Citizens of the towns and ranchers, where the trouble centered, turned over their firearms and ammunition to the union men and they were able to repel the attacks of Colorado's uniformed murderers.

Three union men were killed after the Ludlow massacre, two at Aguilar and one at Walsenburg.

The militia used every means of deception to defeat the strikers and influence public opinion against them.

At Walsenburg, Major P. P. Lester, a Red Cross officer, went on the firing line when the fight started on "the hogback."

He was killed while engaged in the fighting. But the militia told a different story. They gave their prostituted newspapers a sob story of how the strikers had killed a Red Cross officer when he was ministering to the wounded.

The militia at first announced that only one of their men had been killed in the fighting. Since that time five more bodies have been found.

Probably the most vicious fighting after Ludlow occurred at Forbes, almost two weeks later.

For months the militia and gunmen had been attempting to "clean out" that colony. March 10, when Neil Smith, a negro strikebreaker, got drunk and was killed by a train, Czar Chase found an excuse for destroying the lower tent colony at Forbes. He said that Smith had been murdered by the strikers. He destroyed the miners' homes, threw them out into a blinding snowstorm without food or shelter, but he did not "clean out" the strikers.

The night before the federal troops came into the strike zone the murderous mine guards decided to make one last attempt to do this work. They attacked the strikers. But the union men and their families had long been expecting just such an attack, and when the battle was over nine gunmen and scabs were dead and part of the Forbes mine destroyed.

Chase Defends Thugs.

Since the Ludlow massacre, the state militia and Adjutant General John Chase have done everything in their power to discredit the strikers and to counteract the revolting protest of the people of the

GOVERNOR ELIAS M. AMMONS, SPINELESS TOOL OF THE
COAL OPERATORS

United States against the murder of women and children.

Chase himself has become an evangelist in the interest of the "Law and Order League," a body boosted by prostituted sheets of the operators and which stands for anything that will enable the corporations to own, body and soul, everything in the state of Colorado, from its wonderful natural resources down to the ignorant men of foreign nations whom they may import to dig wealth for them.

Former Judge Advocate Major E. J. Boughton, notorious tool of the Cripple Creek operators, has been sent east by Chase, or Cheese, as you will, to tell the people that no women and children were killed at Ludlow.

Following the report of the military committee on its findings in the Ludlow affair, a court martial has been held, a real dignified court martial, the members of which have for years taken the championship of the whitewash league.

Every truth long since established by the coal miners and representative citizens has been denied by the imported assassins of the operators, or, let us say, the Colorado National Guard.

Newspapers of the state began to talk of the "whitewash," so the military court martial decided that there must be a "goat." Lieut. (Butcher) K. E. Linderfelt was selected. He testified that he struck Louis Tikas on the head and broke the stock of his gun. But he said Louis had cursed him for murdering the women and children. Knowing the personnel of the court martial, citizens of Colorado expect that Linderfelt will probably be punished "severely" by the militia for the murder of Tikas. As a matter of fact, these citizens believe that the court martial officials, or operators' tools, as you wish, will decide that in the murder of Louis Tikas, Linderfelt was guilty of conduct unbecoming an officer and may censure him severely.

Since the federal troops arrived there has been no disturbance, except during the last week in May, when several gunmen attacked the United States troops.

The coal barons went at once to the officers and blamed it on the strikers.

It was just another example of the hysterical, malicious efforts of the operators to discredit the strikers.

The operators said it was evident that strikers fired the shots since' they came from their tent colony. To one not acquainted with methods of the coal barons this would seem reasonable. But the people of Colorado remember the dynamite which the strikers were supposed to have planted and exploded at Sopris to terrorize the neighborhood. For months the union men were charged with these acts of lawlessness.

And then came the congressional investigation. The coal barons called Tony Langowski to prove that the strikers were responsible. Tony told of how the operators had paid him $3 a day to join the union as a spotter. He said he had become secretary of the Sopris local and received $3 a week from the union.

Spotters Terrorize Towns.

But he did not tell the story the operators put him on the stand to tell. He said that all of these dynamite explosions had been deliberately planned and carried out by the spotters of the operators in the union to throw discredit on the real striking coal miners.

If the shots did come from the strikers' colony, citizens of Colorado are convinced that they were fired by another Tony Langowski in the pay of the coal operators.

As long as the coal mines where the trouble centers are allowed to run with imported scabs and gunmen, there is certain to be bloodshed unless the federal troops are kept in the field.

That Ammons has not completed his work for the coal operators and still hopes to serve them by trying again to break the strike with the state militia was shown by the special session of the state legislature.

The legislators were called together by Ammons to provide means of paying the $700,000 military debt contracted by him and his lickspittle partner of the coal operators, John Chase, in their attempt to break the strike.

A saloonkeeper and gambler and notorious tool of the operators was elected speaker of the house, and when the legislature adjourned its members had passed a $1,000,000 appropriation bill, providing $300,000 to send the militia back into the strike district to carry on their work of intimidation and terror if the federal troops are withdrawn.

The people of Colorado know what this state militia did before the Ludlow massacre.

They know how they attempted to slaughter women with babes in their arms on the streets of Trinidad January 22, 1914; they know how they robbed and plundered and destroyed homes; they know how they insulted and abused and outraged women; they know how they denied men and women their constitutional rights, filled jails with innocent strikers and held them incommunicado as military prisoners and committed countless other outrages in their effort to break the spirit of the strikers.

They know that if the federal troops are removed and the militia returned to the field, the state troopers will carry on their work of carnage in a vain effort to break the strike.

As long as the federal troops remain in the field, peace will continue as far as the strikers are concerned.

POLICY COMMITTEE OF THE UNITED MINE WORKERS OF AMERICA.

Reading left to right—John McLennan, President District 15; E. L. Doyle. Secretary-Treasurer District 15; John R. Lawson, International Board Member District 15; Frank J. Hayes, International Vice-President.

Only the future can tell what is to be the fate of the Colorado strikers and their wives and children.

The Ludlow massacre and the Colorado situation as it stands today is a gruesome prophecy to labor men of the world.

They need but realize that the Colorado coal miners have suffered all of the outrages mentioned in this book and many more in a fight to secure an enforcement of the laws of the state of Colorado, to realize what may be their fate in the future.

Causes of the Strike

The bloody massacre of twenty-one men, women
.and children at Ludlow, Colo., April 20, 1914, was
the final effort of the coal operators and John D.
Rockefeller to wipe out every vestige of the labor
movement in Colorado and to give warning to any
who might·demand their constitutional rights that
theirs would be a similar fate.

For more than thirty years the coal miners of
Colorado have been only so many slaves of the
operators. Every industrial, political and religious
right has been denied them. Legislation in the interests of the workers has availed them nothing, for
the coal companies have owned the courts.

As early as 1884 the miners banded themselves
together in an effort to get those rights granted
them by the constitution of the United States and
the statutes of Colorado. Each time, however, by
murdering them, by burning their homes, by deport-
ing them, and other high-handed methods the operators were able to break the strike.

In 1904 the miners made their most valiant
effort to break their bondage. For months and
months they fought, suffered untold privations,
only in the end to be deported from Colorado like
so many cattle in box cars.

Immediately after that strike was called off,
6,000 men who had belonged to the union were
blacklisted. Some of the mine owners opposed this
policy, but were forced to carry it out through the
absolute domination of the state by Rockefeller and
the larger corporations. If they refused to obey the
mandates of the triumvirate, certain ruin was the
result. Sometimes their credit was stopped at the
banks. At other times the Rockefeller gang would
go into their market and undersell them as much as
one dollar a ton. Other methods were used and
always successfully, with the result that no matter

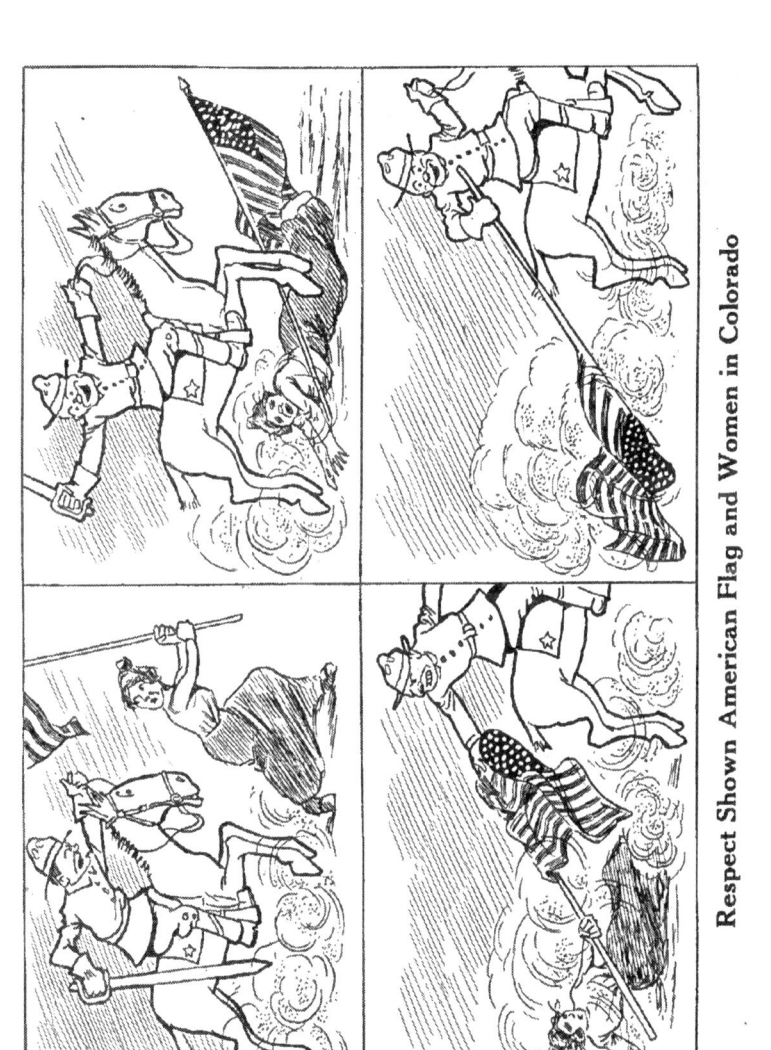

Respect Shown American Flag and Women in Colorado

how a man might feel toward his men he must submit to the tyrannies of the larger companies.

The oppressions of the men which led up to the present strike are so foreign to American liberty that they are almost unbelievable to the man who believes that constitutional government does exist everywhere in this supposed land of the free. But men who have suffered them for years have absolutely established them as facts before the congressional committee which recently investigated the Colorado strike, and they must be believed.

Operators Break Laws.

One of the many laws passed in the interests of the miners is that providing for a checkweighman. This has been a statute for a decade, but the miners have never been allowed a checkweighman. Here and there men robbed of 700 to 1,400 pounds of coal on every car they mined would get together and demand their state right to have a checkweighman. They were discharged at once.

The abolition of the scrip system, the granting of the right to trade wherever they pleased, to belong to a union, and the establishing of a semi-monthly pay-day, are other laws and rights passed by the Colorado legislature, but which the operators have always denied the men.

The miners of Colorado have never been allowed their political rights. On election day they were driven like so many sheep to the polls. The superintendent sent one man in to vote. He marked a ballot, but instead of placing it in the box took it to the superintendent. This was given to a man to place in the ballot box, and he in turn brought out a ballot marked in the same way. Thus the endless chain was continued. Any man who refused to vote was discharged and driven out of the county. At times when even this method would not win an election, some prominent man was arrested. His friends were told that he would be "fixed" if they did not make his followers vote the way of the coal operators.

If the coal operators wanted to "get" anyone and they did get everyone suspected of even being a union sympathizer, the sheriff in either Las Animas or Huerfano counties did the work. Men were arrested on trumped-up charges and tried by fixed juries. An example of the rotten conditions in Huerfano County was given the congressional investigating committee. Louis Miller, a notorious thug and deputy sheriff, assaulted a union man, breaking his jaw. The miner had Miller arrested He was tried and acquitted by a jury, seven of whom were likewise deputy sheriffs.

Lawson Persecuted.

The case of John R. Lawson, international board member of the United Mine Workers of America, shows how rotten is the government in the strike district and how they "get" union men whether there is anything against them or not.

In 1906, Lawson went into Huerfano county to organize the miners. The operators spotted him at once and ordered the sheriff to "get" Lawson.

But the labor leader broke no laws. The coal barons finally became frantic to think that there was a union man at large in their midst informing the men of their constitutional rights, and ordered the sheriff to "get" Lawson or get out himself.

So, one night Lawson left Walsenburg to visit a nearby mining camp. Two thugs of the sheriff followed him. When Lawson reached the edge of the town, one of the thugs stepped up to him. Another put a six-shooter in the union man's pocket and the first "police" officer arrested Lawson for carrying concealed deadly weapons.

The union organizer was placed in jail and held there.

Strikebreakers brought in from every section of Europe and Japan to take the places of the blacklisted and deported miners of the 1904 strike soon began to realize that Huerfano and Las Animas counties, Colorado, were not a part of the United States—that constitutional government did not exist there. They, too, began to clamor for their rights. They received their discharge and were sent "down the canyon."

They realized that only by organization could they hope to obtain their constitutional rights and they began petitioning the United Mine Workers of America to organize them. Finally in 1911 organizers were sent into the district, only to be beaten up and driven out.

11,232 Men Strike.

Conditions finally became so unbearable that the miners sent delegates to a convention at Trinidad, Colorado, September 16, 1913. They demanded to strike at once, but cooler heads of the Mine Workers insisted that they give the operators a week in which to meet with them and discuss their grievances. The coal barons refused to meet their men, and September 23, 1913, 11,232 men left their work in a fight to a finish to get the seven demands drawn up at the Trinidad convention. All of these with the exception of a slight increase in wages are granted by the laws of the state.

When the operators saw a strike was inevitable the Baldwin Feltz detective agency was employed, and hundreds of gunmen and hired assassins, many of whom had murdered women and children in the West Virginia strike, were brought into the state. More than a dozen machine guns were purchased and a systematic reign of terror that has known no equal in the history of industrial conflicts was begun by these hired murderers of John D. Rockefeller. Gerald Lippiatt was the first to pay the death pen-

ORDERS

alty. He was murdered in the streets of Trinidad August 16, 1913.

One of the most dastardly death-dealing devices employed by the coal barons to harrass, intimidate and murder the strikers was a high-powered automobile covered with armor plate and mounted with a machine gun and six thugs with high-powered rifles.

Death Special at Work.

During the day this "Death Special" was driven at top speed through the strike zone, shooting into the tent colonies. One of the most nefarious acts of these hired murderers of industry was the attack on the Forbes tent colony of peaceful strikers. On the afternoon of October 17 the strikers were aroused from the quiet monotony of their existence by the approach of an automobile. They crowded to the entrance to the colony to meet a man who came toward them bearing a white flag. The leader of the strikers went to greet him. The gunman exhibited a union card and asked the men whether they too belonged to the union. They said they did. "Well, if you do, you'd better look out," said he. The gunman dropped the flag and the shooting began. A whistling reign of bullets scattered the men and women to every possible place of safety. But the bullets were faster than humans. One man was killed and a young boy received nine bullet wounds in the leg while he was trying to crawl into his tent.

In these tented cities of the strikers were hundreds of mothers with babes at their breasts, men, women and children braving the elements, the hardships of life, but happy in the belief that the dawn of a happier civilization was at hand. When the children went to play in the day, mothers and fathers never knew whether their homes would be destroyed before their return nor whether the happy little future citizens of the United States would meet the terrible fate suffered by the residents of Ludlow at the hands of the gunmen.

And if the day did pass without slaughter, the night was spent in equal terror of these imported assassins. On every point of vantage surrounding the tent colonies the operators placed searchlights. The panic among the strikers and their families which they had kept up during the day was continued at night by the searchlight. These powerful machines were played on the tent colonies from dusk to dawn, making it impossible for the strikers to sleep and keeping them in constant fear of an attack by machine guns and high-powered rifles, which might come at any moment from the gunmen who make their living by murdering and terrorizing their brothers and sisters.

In October the operators, who own Huerfano County, placed some of their thugs with a machine gun in Walsenburg. It was turned loose on the unarmed and peaceful strikers who lined the street. When the smoke cleared away four members of the United Mine Workers had paid the penalty of fighting for their constitutional rights in Colorado.

Gunmen Murder Eleven.

When the state militia was called out October 27, 1913, eleven striking coal miners had been killed by these murderers of John D. Rockefeller and his subordinates, the Colorado coal operators.

But if the gunmen were murderers, if they were robbers, if they were abusers of women, they were better than the Colorado National Guard, under the command of John Chase, who, drunk with the flattery of his bosses, the operators, and intoxicated with an ill-founded idea of his own importance, stopped at nothing in his effort to break the strike of the coal miners.

It is impossible to tell in a few lines of the atrocities of the so-called militiamen, many of whom were recruited from the civic cesspools of the world and the Baldwin Feltz hired assassins.

Constitutional government was absolutely set aside by the state militia. The case of Mother Jones, 82-year-old angel of the coal camps, illustrates the truth of this statement.

When the strike started, Mother Jones was on the scene doing all in her power to help the women and children. During this time she did much to keep the men of the strike colonies orderly and law-abiding.

When the militia went into the field and started its reign of terror, Mother Jones denounced their actions in no uncertain terms. During the latter part of December she stopped in Trinidad on her way from El Paso to Denver. She was deported at once by the militia.

For months Elias M. Ammons, lickspittle of the coal operators and cattle-puncher, but bearing the title of governor of Colorado, had threatened to arrest Mother Jones if she attempted to enter the strike zone.

Mother Jones in Bull Pen.

Determined that she would exercise her constitutional right to go where and when she pleased, Mother Jones eluded three thugs who were spotting her and went to Trinidad, Sunday evening, January 11th.

One hundred and fifty militiamen stormed the Toltec hotel shortly before noon the next day and succeeded in making her a military prisoner. She was taken to San Rafael hospital, which was turned into a military bastile, and held incommunicado for nine weeks.

Through the United Mine Workers' attorney, Horace N. Hawkins, she applied to the state supreme

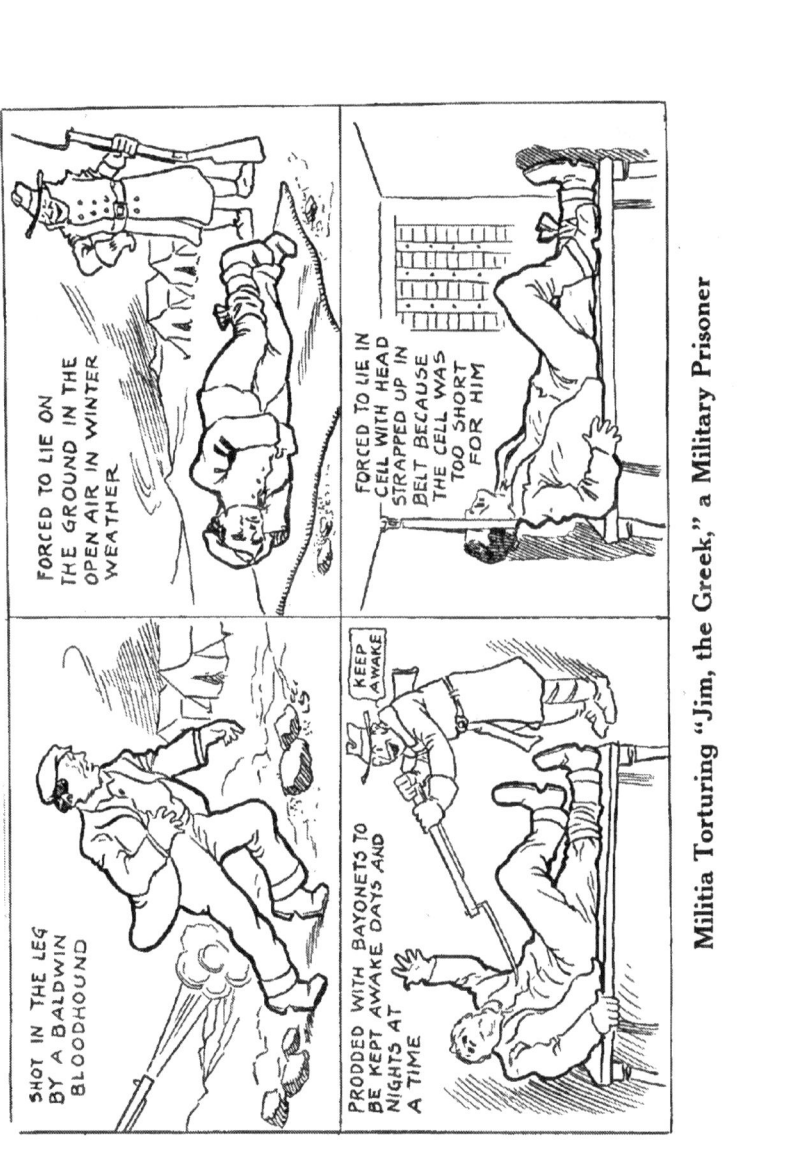

Militia Torturing "Jim, the Greek," a Military Prisoner

court for a writ of habeas corpus. Before the court
could hand down a decision, the militiamen went to
her with the announcement that Governor Ammons
desired to talk to her. When she reached Denver the
militia gave out the statement that she had asked to
come to Denver and that she was no longer a prisoner, thus forestalling a possible reversal of the
notorious Moyer decision.

A week later she returned to the strike zone and
this time was kidnapped from the train at Walsenburg and thrown into a vermin-ridden cellar cell in
the Huerfano county jail.

Finally the supreme court issued the writ of
habeas corpus, ordering the militia to show cause
why she should not be liberated. But the militia
again prevented a reversal of the Moyer decision by
releasing her before the date of hearing set by the
supreme court.

The Colorado militia went wild in their efforts
to break the strike. They interfered with the United
States mail, with United States officials, and prevented state officers from carrying out their regular
work of inspecting the mines.

One of the many instances of the latter was had
when State Factory Inspectors Eli Gross, Frank
Mancini and George Howe went to Delagua and Hastings to learn whether the men were being held in
the mines against their will.

When company and militia officers learned that
Mancini, who is editor of an Italian paper favorable
to the miners, was in the party, they refused them
admittance to the mine.

To add to this outrage, Major Hamrock, saloonkeeper, officer of the militia and later in charge of
the Ludlow murderers of women, children and un-
born babes, tried to make political capital out of the
incident by deliberately lying when he said that Mancini had told him he had orders from Deputy Labor

Commissioner E. V. Brake to get the men out of the mines.

Homes Plundered.

Homes were broken into on the pretense that these militiamen were searching for arms. They had no search warrants. The authority of Rockefeller's approval, or the state of Colorado, as you please, was sufficient warrant for their plundering expeditions, and they stole everything of value.

One of the most pitiful stories told the congressional investigating committee was that of a little son of Mrs. Yankinski. She had gone to town, leaving her four little children alone in the house. Along came a militiaman and his captain, the latter lying on the seat in a drunken stupor. The militiaman entered and began a search. He finally found $200 sewed in the hem of an old coat. The little boy was prostrated when he saw the "soldier" was going to take the money and was rewarded with a punch on the jaw. When he fell from the blow the gunman-militiaman kicked him in the face. A younger sister began to cry when she saw that her brother had been hurt, and she too was knocked down. The robber kicked her in the face, breaking her nose. The incident happened several days before the congressional investigating committee arrived in the strike zone, but the child's nose was so seriously fractured that she was unable to testify before the congressman.

Over in Segundo a woman was taking one of her children to visit relatives. A drunken militiaman took the child from her, made the tot line up with other children, and then forced the procession of children to march about the city for two hours while he jabbed them now and then with a bayonet to make them realize that they were marching on the orders of one of the "peace-preservers" of the capitalistic-ridden state of Colorado.

Women Outraged.

Someone fired a shot at Aguilar one night. Two militiamen saw several women come out of a back gate. They grabbed them and dragged both through a snow-covered alley to the jail. One of these women was to become a mother in a few hours. She fainted, but that did not prevent the scab-herding militia of the state of Colorado from putting her through the notorious third degree When a doctor informed the "arm of Colorado law" that the mother might at any moment give birth to the child, the woman was released and allowed to go to her home. It was later proved that the shots were fired by some of the gunmen militiamen in an attempt to start a battle and murder the strikers and their wives and children.

Saloonkeepers were also favorite subjects of torture for the militiamen. In Segundo one night four militiamen went to the door of a saloon after twelve o'clock at night. They demanded admittance and were refused. Guns belonging to the state of Colorado, or Rockefeller, were put into use, the door battered in, the saloonkeeper knocked unconscious. After becoming intoxicated, they left the unconscious saloonkeeper on the floor, and carried out all the liquor their arms would hold. Other saloons were robbed and the proprietors beaten up, but no action against them has ever been brought by the state.

Mothers and Babes Maimed.

One of the most notorious outrages of the military rule in the strike district occurred January 22. Mother Jones had been placed in a military bastile because she insisted that as an American citizen she had a right to come and go where and when she pleased. The women of Trinidad and the strike zone decided to hold a protest parade. They went to Adjutant General Chase. He approved their

MILITARISM

The above picture shows Mother Jones, 82-year-old angel of the coal camps, confined in a damp, filthy, cold, cellar cell in the Walsenburg, Colo, jail. She was kidnaped, taken from a train while on her way to Trinidad, and placed in this cell to be held incommunicado as a military prisoner. Her announcement that she intended to exercise her constitutional right as an American citizen to go where and when she pleased was the only reason given by the $700,000 militia for this outrage. This same cell is so uninhabitable that it caused the death of a healthy young Greek, who contracted rheumatism of the heart.

line of march and the parade was held. Down the
street they went, little children trotting beside their
mothers carrying babes at their breast. Nothing
could have been more orderly. Suddenly down the
street rushed the mounted troopers of the state of
Colorado with sabers drawn. At their head was
Chase. Women and children were trampled under
the hoofs of the horses, mothers were slashed with
sabers, more than a dozen of them being mutilated.

But if this was a horrible outrage, it did not
equal the bloodthirsty actions of this inhuman
despot, Chase. Sarah Slator, a 16-year-old girl, was
returning from school. When she saw the attempted
wholesale massacre of women and children she
stopped to see the trouble. Chase, a man clothed
with the full military authority of the state of Colorado, rode up and ordered her to move on. Her
feet could not move fast enough to please the bloodthirsty military tool of the coal operators, and the
general of the militia of the state of Colorado
kicked this little innocent school girl in the breast
so savagely that she may never be able to nurse a
babe.

Nothing was left undone by the militiamen to
prove that they were no more than the employes of
the coal operators. For months they threatened to
"clean out the tent colonies and every d—— rough
red-neck in them." They could find no excuse. One
night a negro strikebreaker got drunk and went to
sleep on a railroad track near Suffield. He was run
over and killed by an approaching train. Foxhounds
were placed on the trial of the "murderer." They
went the opposite direction from the Forbes tent
colony. No proof could be fastened on strikers by
going this way, so the militia thugs led the hounds
into the Forbes tent colony. The news was flashed
to the world that bloodhounds had tracked the
"murderer" to the Forbes colony. The Colorado-
clothed fiends demolished the tent colony, throwing

the men, women and children out into a blinding
snowstorm, with the nearest place of shelter several
miles away.   Sixteen of the strikers were arrested
for the murder of the drunken strikebreaker who
was killed by a train.

Miners Held Incommunicado.

One of the favorite methods used by the militia
in their attempt to break the strike was to arrest
union officials and strikers by the wholesale without
warrant or charge and hold them incommunicado.
In jail they were subjected to untold·torture and
threatened with all kinds of violent deaths unless
they implicated high officials of the United Mine
Workers in some crime.   For five and six nights at
a time these poor strikers were kept awake by bayonet jabs and dashes of cold water.

It was these and hundreds of other tyrannies
and outrages practised on the men, women and children of the strike zone that led up to the horrible
massacre of innocents at Ludlow, April 20.

The militia, after incurring a debt of $1,000,000
on the state to aid the coal operators, had been
withdrawn the Thursday before.   They had no
sooner been taken from the field than all the hired
murderers of the coal operators in that district
were recruited into the militia.   These assassins
were stationed at Ludlow under command of Major
Pat Hamrock and Lieutenant Karl E. Linderfelt,
who for months had threatened to clean out all the
tent colonies and ''murder every d—— one of those
red-necks.''·

The cause of the entire trouble in Colorado was
summarized by Judge Ben B. Lindsey of Denver
when he testified before the Committee on Industrial
Relations in New York City.

He said: ''Colorado has perfected the science
of corrupting men.   Its judges, its supreme court

judge, are owned like the office boy; its business men, its lawyers, are all owned.

"Capitalists in Colorado have carried out most perfidious deals to control the agencies of the laws, and not only make laws, but prevent the enforcement of laws."

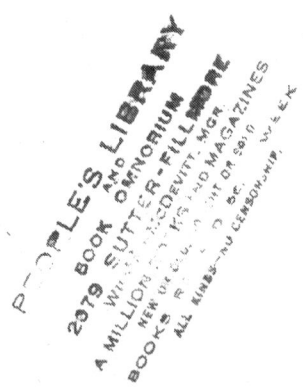

JUSTICE IN COLORADO

The Massacre of the Innocents

(The Rocky Mountain News)

(Note—The following editorial appeared in the
News April 22, 1914, two days after the Ludlow horror. Prior to that time the News had favored the
operators.)

The horror of the shambles at Ludlow is over-
whelming. Not since the days when pitiless red men
wreaked vengeance upon intruding frontiersmen and
upon their women and children has this western
country been stained with so foul a deed.

The details of the massacre are horrible. Mexico offers no barbarity so base as that of the murder
of defenseless women and children by the mine
guards in soldiers' clothing. Like whitened sepul-
chres we boast of American civilization with this
infamous thing at our very doors. Huerta murdered
Madero, but even Huerta did not shoot an innocent·
little boy seeking water for his mother who lay ill.
Villa is a barbarian, but in his maddest excess Villa
has not turned machine guns on imprisoned women
and children. Where is the outlaw so far beyond
the pale of human kind as to burn the tent over the
heads of nursing mothers and helpless little babies?

Out of this infamy one fact stands clear. Machine guns did the murder. The machine guns were
in the hands of mine guards, most of whom were
also members of the militia. It was a private war,
with the wealth of the richest man in the world behind the mine guards.

Once and for all time the right to employ armed
guards must be taken away from private individuals
and corporations. To the state, and to the state
alone, belongs the right to maintain peace. Anything else is anarchy. Private warfare is the only
sort of anarchy the world has ever known, and armed
forces employed by private interests have introduced

the only private wars of modern times. This practice must be stopped. If the state laws are not strong enough, then the federal government must step in. At any cost, private warfare must be destroyed.

Who are these mine guards to whom is entrusted the sovereign right to massacre? Four of the fraternity were electrocuted recently in New York. They are the gunmen of the great cities, the offscourings of humanity, whom a bitter heritage has made the wastrels of the world. Warped by the wrongs of their own upbringing, they know no justice and they care not for mercy. They are hardly human in intelligence, and not as high in the scale of kindness as domestic animals.

Yet they are not the guilty ones. The blood of the innocent women and children rests on the hands of those who for the greed of dollars employed such men and bought such machines of murder. The world has not been hard upon these; theirs has been a gentle upbringing. Yet they reck not of human life when pecuniary interests are involved.

The blood of the women and children, burned and shot like rats, cries aloud from the ground. The great state of Colorado has failed them. It has betrayed them. Her militia, which should have been the impartial protectors of the peace have acted as murderous gunmen. The machine guns which played in the darkness upon the homes of humble men and women, whose only crime was an effort to earn an honest living, were bought and paid for by agents of the mine owners. Explosive bullets have been used on children. Does the bloodiest page in the French revolution approach this in hideousness?

In the name of humanity, in the name of civilization, we have appealed to President Wilson. His ear heard the wail of the innocent, outraged and dying in Mexico. Cannot the president give heed to the sufferings of his own people?

Think, Mr. President, of the captain of the strikers, Louis Tikas, whose truce with the gunmen was ended with his murder. Think of the fifty-one shots which were passed through the strike leader. Think of his body, which has lain exposed since his infamous killing. Then, with that vast power which has been committed to you as the executive of a great nation, attend to the misery wrought by an anarchistic lust for dollars. Without your speedy aid the poor and the needy, betrayed by the state, may be slaughtered to the last smiling babe.

THE "DEATH SPECIAL" OF THE COLORADO COAL OPERATORS
The armored automobile, equipped with a machine gun and manned by
six Baldwin-Feltz murderers, who murdered and intimidated the strikers
during the early part of the strike.

Printed in the USA
CPSIA information can be obtained
at www.ICGtesting.com
LVHW011115190324
774895LV00008B/270